John J. Tigert, G. W. Wilson

The Council Meeting

John J. Tigert, G. W. Wilson

The Council Meeting

ISBN/EAN: 9783337302054

Printed in Europe, USA, Canada, Australia, Japan

Cover: Foto ©Andreas Hilbeck / pixelio.de

More available books at **www.hansebooks.com**

THE COUNCIL MEETING.

BY THE REV. G. W. WILSON,

Of the Memphis Conference.

———

EDITED, WITH AN INTRODUCTION, BY JNO. J. TIGERT, LL.D.,

Book Editor, Methodist Episcopal Church, South.

———

PRINTED FOR THE AUTHOR
BY THE PUBLISHING HOUSE OF THE M. E. CHURCH, SOUTH.
BARBEE & SMITH, AGENTS, NASHVILLE, TENN.
1897.

CONTENTS.

(iii)

INTRODUCTION.

THE following pages well illustrate how widely and beneficently the influence of an alert and wise presiding elder can be extended by conveying needed information and suggestion to all the church officers entitled to seats in the Quarterly Conference. The local traditions and customs of a circuit sometimes override the distinct provisions of the Discipline. The people may not perish for lack of spiritual knowledge; but the work of the Church sometimes lags or fails for the lack of business or legal knowledge, much of which can be gathered from a careful study of our form of Discipline. Church officers of every kind and grade should be familiar with the pages of that wonderful little book, and one excellent result of Brother Wilson's practical and pertinent suggestions in this pamphlet will be to send local preachers, stewards, trustees, and other officers to the Discipline itself, in which the following pages cannot fail to arouse an intelligent interest.

The presiding eldership is a useful and indispensable arm of the service. Let the incumbents magnify the office, taking a real oversight of all the interests of the Church in their districts, and a helpful direction of all the officers, and we shall hear fewer quadrennial suggestions of its modification. I cordially commend the thoughtful perusal of the following pages to all those for whom they have been so carefully and ably prepared.

JNO. J. TIGERT.

NASHVILLE, 13 *October*, 1897.

THE COUNCIL MEETING.

CHAPTER I.

WHILE holding Quarterly Conferences over our district and enjoying association with the people on other occasions, I observed some conditions which doubt-less are common among other districts of our enlarging Church; and they share these conditions with us in varying degrees: a want of information, and a consequent lack of appreciation of obligations to God, the Church, and the world; also a consequent looseness in the temporal interests of the Church. It is with the hope of being helpful that we offer this little book to the kind consideration of any into whose hands it may fall, wishing, too, that it may carry special encouragement into the homes where we have found such friendly hospitality. While the first two or three pages pertain specially to our own field of labor, we try to make this, as the remaining part of the book, of interest to our people everywhere.

The general condition of the district has been slowly improving for quite a while, and in some respects it is now better than ever before. Any advancement whatever is encouraging, but the improvement is not sufficient to induce ecstasy. Sometimes figures may not be entertaining, while they may be quite disclosing. The information given in the following table I gather from the "Minutes" of our Annual Conference for 1896, our last session. The first columns compare our eight districts, and show that, while the

(1)

Paris District has more members than *any* other, and
two thousand above some of them, in other interests
it is behind every other, except the Lexington District,
and that is a mission district. This is not caused by
poverty among our people, but by a want of development—church education—on the part of members
and officials. The other columns show what each pastoral charge in the Paris District did last year in certain obligations. These few items are sufficient to be
suggestive.

MEMPHIS CONFERENCE.

	Number of Members.	Paid for Support of Ministry.	Paid Per Member for Support of Ministry.	Paid for Foreign Missions.	Paid Per Member for Foreign Missions.
Memphis District	7,410	$17,098 92	$2 31	$1,967 50	.26½
Brownsville District	6,673	9,911 04	1 49	1,288 20	.19
Jackson District	6,068	9,742 50	1 61	1,226 98	.20
Dyersburg District	7,803	10,934 24	1 41	1,360 18	.17½
Union City District	8,184	10,280 19	1 26	1,227 97	.15
Paducah District	8 237	10,291 51	1 25	999. 68	.12
Paris District	8.207	8,287 29	1 00	624 30	.07½
Lexington District	6.863	4,811 40	70	280 40	.04

PARIS DISTRICT.

	Number of Members.	Paid for Support of Ministry.	Paid Per Member for Support of Ministry.	Paid for Foreign Missions.	Paid Per Member for Foreign Missions.
Paris Station	335	$1,665 00	$4 97	$135 00	.40¼
Henry Circuit	380	416 47	1 10	20 00	.05¼
McKenzie Station	248	800 00	3 22	120 00	.48
McKenzie Circuit	601	520 07	86	29 00	.05
Atwood Circuit	422	319 39	75	15 00	.08½
Gleason and Liberty	257	333 99	1 30	50 00	.19½
Manlyville Circuit	602	403 88	67	22 15	.03⅔
Big Sandy Circuit	532	228 14	42	10 00	.02
Conyersville Circuit	560	375 88	67	25 00	.03
Cottage Grove Circuit	426	341 92	80		....
New Providence Circuit	681	339 40	50	35 00	.05
Springville Circuit	298	169 81	57	8 00	.03
Harris Grove Circuit	472	172 60	86	22 00	.05
Murray Circuit	503	775 61	1 54	56 00	.11
Crossland Circuit	600	580 00	97	21 00	.03½
Benton Mission	332	414 10	1 25	35 00	.10
Hico Circuit	652	195 28	30	13 00	.02
Briensburg Circuit	396	281 75	58	8 15	.02

This presentation of the district, I know, will be
mortifying to every member with self-respect and concern for the cause of Christ; but the facts ought to be

known, and such facts should arouse every member in the district, old and young, to extraordinary exertions for proper advancement. Let every one at once do the best possible, regardless of what others may or may not do. Let each pay as much over his assessment as he can, but never less than that; and let all the offi· cials meet their responsibilities as leaders of the Church.

A man has no right to accept any office in the Church, and then make no effort to meet its responsibilities. Upon accepting an office, he is morally bound to make faithful efforts to discharge its obligations; and he has no right to decline the position without good reasons for doing so. Every Christian made a contract with God to do his bidding, and most calls of the Church are providential openings for service. If, after faithful effort, he learns that from any cause whatever he cannot or will not perform the duties of the office, he ought at the next Quarterly Conference to resign and let a more efficient man be put in his place. If an unfaithful officer will not amend or voluntarily resign, the Quarterly Conference ought to displace him under the second question, "Are there any complaints?" and, if they can, elect another who will care for the Church. If the Quarterly Conference suffers the Church imposed upon by continued negligence of indifferent officials, they themselves become culpable. The Church suffers as much from neglect as from any other cause whatever. Every officer and every Methodist family should have a copy of the last edition of our Discipline, and study it specially to learn his own duties. It is great folly for any man to assume, upon his election, that he understands all the work incident to his office, civil or ecclesiastical. He should study his work, magnify his office, whatever it be, and extend his usefulness. Every member is as certainly obilgated to perform certain duties as any minister is bound to preach the gospel. An official should attend his Quarterly Meetings, unless unavoidably prevented. Some superintendents, trustees, secretaries of Church Conferences, and even stewards, seldom attend their Quarterly Conference; some never attend. This is *the business* meeting of their pastoral charge; and they should be there to assume their own part of the Church work, help plan for its interests, encourage others by their counsel and presence, instead of discouraging them by their absence; learn all they can, catch enthusiasm needed, and help impart the same to others.

Brother Henry Pafford, of Big Sandy Circuit, has attended, on his own circuit, one hundred and fifty-six Quarterly Conferences in succession. Brother M. B. Towery, local preacher, of Hico Circuit, has missed only one of his own Quarterly Conferences for thirty-eight years. He was really at that, but was called away to the bedside of a dying neighbor. Many others attend regularly, and never leave till the Quarterly Conference is adjourned, and are otherwise loyal and useful. Most fortunately for us, God, in his providence, has distributed these helpful men, so that every charge in the district has some. There are encouraging signs of improvement; and if all concerned will adopt and practice the principles suggested in this paragraph, they will enjoy a most desirable revolution within twelve months. Some of the official boards have already begun to put these suggestions into practice.

The Council Meetings are held with the special purpose of acquainting our leaders and other members with the duties and prerogatives of the Quarterly Conference officials and to induce needed enthusiasm. The preacher in charge invites one or two neighboring pastors, and appoints several of his most efficient leaders to first study, then in the " meeting " discuss, these subjects. For this work we have an hour or more before preaching, then some time following dinner, and before Quarterly Conference. These Council Meetings are held during our " third round." When properly announced and emphasized and provided for, they have proved most interesting, instructive, and stimulating, and they were well attended; yet a number of our officers were never present. Such failure is to be deplored, but it should not discourage those who are concerned.

These meetings suggested the character and title of this pamphlet. The same obligations of attendance obtain in reference to District Conference. Any man accepting election as delegate to District Conference should attend its session if possible, and should remain there till final adjournment. If some men were as indifferent to other public interests as they are to responsibilities the Church has placed upon them, they would never be honored a second time by the suffrage of an intelligent and thoughtful people.

Our District Conference in 1895, in Paris, was quite a success; that in Benton, in 1896, was far better; that in Maury, this year, was better still. One hundred and ten members of the Conference were present. Enthusiastic interest was sustained to the close. Everything done was edifying, even the disclosure of defects and neglect of work; yet a number of our delegates were absent. We will try to do better next year, if we all be here.

I love thy Church, O God!

.   .   .   .   .

For her my tears shall fall,
For her my prayers ascend;
To her my cares and toils be given,
Till toils and cares shall end.

CHAPTER II.

The Discipline, in Paragraphs 105 and 106, answers the question, "What are the duties of a bishop?" " To see that the districts be formed according to his judgment; . . . to divide a circuit, station, or mission into two or more when he judges it necessary." The only right in shaping charges the Discipline provides for any layman is expressed in Paragraph 190, where, in giving the duties of stewards, it says: " To give advice, if asked, in planning the circuit." Any number of laymen cannot alter the arrangement. Do you think that is putting too much power in the appointing authorities, the bishops (the presiding elders, by usage, being his counselors)? What do you think of Paragraph 321?—" The salary and traveling expenses of preachers on circuits and stations shall be estimated by their respective boards of stewards, after consultation with the preacher in charge." Thus cessions of rights are made by laymen and by preachers, each having confidence in the integrity of the other; and they make the sacrifice for the cause of God, not considering selfish ends, which control all *commercial* interests. The uppermost purpose is to glorify God and save souls. No circuit is ever planned without careful inquiry and consideration first on the part of those intrusted with such work. The wishes of any member will be heard and considered, and the judgment of the wisest is generally sought. Even then the best arrangement may not, at first, be made. In such case patience and confidence and fidelity and sweetness of temper should be practiced till those in authority

(6)

may have time to accomplish the most desirable plans. Sometimes the interests of several neighboring circuits must be considered. Rebellion on the part of any who may be displeased should never be thought of. They have a right to withdraw from the Church when they are displeased, provided their life has been consistent, but no right to rebel in the Church and cause discord among our people. The Discipline clearly provides for the treatment of members for " inveighing against either our doctrines or discipline." (See Paragraph 297.) To take vengeance on the appointing authorities or their counselors, the presiding elders, is wicked, and must be repented of before the crossing of the last river.

Sometimes disaffection among a people is caused by the appointment of a certain preacher to them. A preacher, under our system, would be unfortunate indeed if his reception on a charge depended on his pleasing every one and if a few should be allowed to reject him. " It is estimated that only about seventy-five per cent of the members of a Methodist charge, and so in other denominations, are fully suited to the pastor and he to them." If the chronic grumblers be allowed the reins, a preacher could never feel secure.

A fundamental principle of our system is that, in joining the itinerancy, a preacher, for the cause of God, consents for the bishop (and presiding elders, really) to make his appointments, and waives the privilege of selecting or rejecting his pastoral charge; and the people, in joining our Church, consent, for the cause of God, that the same authorities shall appoint to them preachers; and they waive the claims of selecting or rejecting their pastors. If they rebel against any preacher whomsoever authoritatively sent them, they violate their solemn vows of Church membership to " be subject to the Discipline of the Church," and

do that which, if allowed, would soon ruin our itinerancy and seriously damage, if not destroy, our Church
government. When members are unwilling to submit to our government, as our preachers do, they
should at once withdraw from the Church. They
need not hope, however, to find in any other Christian
denomination a government equal to ours in ministerial supply and spread of the gospel. Our system,
however, as others, is subject to abuse; and, with that,
hurt to all concerned is the result. The wishes of our
preachers and people in this matter are carefully considered and accommodated by the appointing authorities, as far as may be best; but they cannot gratify the
wishes or meet the interests of any charge or any
preacher to the neglect of others.

Our Discipline provides for necessary changes
among the preachers to be made during the year, but
they must be made by a bishop or presiding elder.
This provision for change was not intended to gratify
the whims of a few fault-finding men who care nothing for crushing the feelings, violating the rights, and.
injuring a preacher's good name, which may be all he
has in this world.

The majority of our people are habitually fond of
their preachers, and do not unkindly criticise them.
One good lady (Sister Dycus, of Palma, Ky.) said:
" Brother Wilson, if I cannot say anything good of
our pastor, I never say anything bad. No one, not
even my husband or children, ever heard me say aught
against any pastor we ever had." Her husband remarked: " That is true."

We have many men and women who get help from
every sermon, and never look for errors; who see and
admire all the noble traits of their worthy pastors, but
never search for faults; and who always furnish their
financial and moral support without a murmur. One

brother, in Quarterly Conference, said to me: " I
stick to my pastor when he is in the right and when he
is in the wrong—all the time. When he is wrong,
like a brother, I try to help him get right. I never
desert him." The editor of the *Christian Standard*
wrote: " We overheard a young woman say not long
ago, ' I do not remember ever to have heard in my
father's home one disrespectful or unkind word concerning a minister.' She paid to her parents a very
high compliment, and described a condition of things
which should find a counterpart in every Christian
home in the land." *Zion's Herald* gave the following incident: "A group of Church people were one
evening discussing the merits of a former pastor, the
weight of criticism being on the unfavorable side. At
last one of the number remarked, ' Well, I don't think
he was much of a preacher, anyway; I never could get
interested in his sermons,' and, appealing to an aged
official brother who was present, and from whom she
expected a sympathetic answer, was immediately si-
lenced by his reply, as follows: ' Well, Sister ——,
the poorest preacher that I ever heard could preach so
much better than I could live that I never feel like
criticising a minister.' "

"A preacher may not be all that he ought to be;
but when a member tries to undermine his reputation,
or in any way lessen the estimate the people have of
him, or in any other way to impede his work in order to
get rid of him, he proves his unworthiness to a place in
the membership of the Church. When a man does
this and the Church silently ignores his conduct, it
becomes a partaker in the work of breaking down the
minister."

Some charges have a few cold-hearted, rule-or-ruin,
fault-finding sort of men, who will, even upon most
trivial grounds, dislike their pastor and develop a sen-

timent against him, while he may be doing the very best work for his charge. They form a little band, who think, at the end of the year, a change in pastors is needed. These are joined by a few whose sins the pastor rightly rebuked; sometimes by a few who think, because he offended one or two, he has ruined himself; or by a few who think a preacher ought never to stay in the same charge longer than one or two years; or by a few who never like to hear the same preacher longer than one year. They are not capable of loving a preacher. (Their poor children must grow up on the food such parents furnish.) So a change of preachers is urged. They never seem to think or care that they may be violating the wishes of their own people and imposing upon them an unsavory reputation and perpetrating a great wrong upon their pastor, who, possibly, has done all of his work faithfully. In their blind effort to accomplish their unreasonable desires they seem never to have heard of the Golden Rule. Every year some such men even go to Conference, and there talk to the irreparable and grievous hurt of their faithful pastor, and seek his removal, when the great body of their people want his return, and, in some cases, are not expecting any change. *"Cruel,"* you say? It would take several adjectives to express the sinfulness of such a sin. Besides, no *unkind* or *unfaithful* member should be recognized in complaints against his pastor, whether at home or at Conference. Honorable officials ought to protect the reputation of their charge and their preacher's good name and interests, and never allow such unfair and damaging representation anywhere. I recommend the course of one of our most useful men of Martin, Tenn. He usually wants his preacher returned; but when he thinks a change necessary, he does not talk promiscuously about it; and he never offers this opinion unless it is of such importance that he can face his pastor with it. Officials ought always to discourage complaints among our people, and never themselves ask for a change of preachers without kindly presenting the matter to the pastor and presiding elder. Then speak of it nowhere else. This course would be with candor and honesty, and would secure the best and most pleasing results. Sometimes a preacher's honor, refinement, self-respect, forbid his making any defense, even when most sinned against. This fact, with other interests involved, should cause every conscientious layman to deal most tenderly with his preacher's good name, and with most loving consideration of the interests and feelings of the wife and children of the self-sacrificing itinerant. Sometimes a preacher *does* make mistakes. The Discipline directs the stewards in such cases to " tell the preachers what they think wrong in them." Then, without making a mountain out of a molehill, but by wisely giving a little brotherly counsel, stewards might prove most helpful. The usefulness of a preacher should increase to the end of his fourth year with a people. Changes come often enough under necessity. Our system easily provides for exigencies; but let no one, because of the ready efficiency of our provision, precipitate an emergency.

2

CHAPTER III.

DISCIPLINE (page 91): " How are the trustees to be appointed? Ans. 1. Except where the laws of the state or territory provide differently, the preacher in charge, or, in his absence, the presiding elder, shall have the right of nomination, subject to the confirmation or rejection of the Quarterly Conference." Paragraph 200: " Trustees of our parsonages, churches, schools, colleges, and universities must be at least twenty-one years of age, and must all be members of our Church when proper persons can be had; otherwise one-third of each board may be elected from without." It is their duty to organize, electing " their own chairman, secretary, and treasurer." (See Paragraph 202.) They are " responsible to the Quarterly Conference, . . . which shall have power to dismiss any of them from office; and they shall be required to present a report of their acts, at least once a year, to the Quarterly Conference." (See Paragraph 203.)

It is the duty of the trustees to protect and otherwise care for the church property intrusted to them. They should see that the purposes of dedication of our churches are observed. (See Discipline, entire page 233.) In the service of dedication the officers of the church address the minister thus: " We present you this house, to be set apart from all unhallowed or common uses, for the worship of Almighty God." The minister says: " We solemnly dedicate it to his service for the reading and expounding of his holy word, the administration of his ordinances, and for all other acts of religious worship." In the prayer the minis-

(12)

ter petitions God: "Preserve this house, which we set apart to thy service, from injury and desecration." In some instances trustees allow political gatherings, etc., in the church. Some allow schools taught in the church, instead of encouraging their people to build a schoolhouse. (Discipline, Par. 544.) This protection of our churches comes from a spirit of reverence for God's house, such as the Bible teaches. All "unhallowed or common uses" of the church develop in our children and people irreverence for the worship of God. Such damaging effect no community can afford to permit.

In making their written report to the Quarterly Conference, the trustees should give proper answers to the "following questions: (1) What is the number of churches and parsonages, and what has been expended on the same during the year? (2) What is the value of the same? (3) Do the deeds contain the trust clauses in the Discipline? (4) Where are the title papers kept? (5) Where are they recorded? (Give office, book, and page.)" (Discipline, Par. 87, Ques. 24.) See Par. 420, to which trustees' report refers: "In all conveyances of ground for the building of houses of worship, or upon which they may have been already built, let the following clause be inserted at the proper place: ' In trust, that said premises shall be used, kept, maintained, and disposed of as a place of divine worship for the use of the ministry and membership of the Methodist Episcopal Church, South, subject to the discipline, usage, and ministerial appointments of said Church, as from time to time authorized and declared by the General Conference of said Church, and the Annual Conference within whose bounds the said premises are situate.'" Par. 431 gives the same direction for securing to the Church its parsonage property.

Every board of trustees, where it *has not* been done, should see at once that the deed to their church property is correct, and that it is recorded, then make to their Quarterly Conference a carefully prepared report, clear, short, without needless statements, yet comprehensive. The chairman of a board of trustees once made to his Quarterly Conference, without even consultation with the other trustees, the following report: " One church Frame bilding 40x60 feet with some 10 winders and 2 dores funished with pulpit and benches valued at $——. A parsonage on neiboring lot with some four rooms finished off with a front porch and a well with a brick walk running west to the front gate valued at $——. This is report of —— church property as skeduled by ——." For good reasons, in giving this to the public, I leave blank where names and valuation of property occur. The report gives only two items the Discipline calls for, and it has some striking peculiarities; yet it shows an honest effort, and that is far better than no report.

Our General Board of Church Extension will not aid a congregation in building a church unless the lot upon which they purpose erecting the house be unconditionally transferred, by proper deed, to the Methodist Episcopal Church, South. If that be a wise rule for the protection of the funds of that board, it would be a wise rule for the protection of other money contributed by our people for building churches, and a security against many probable annoyances and possible disruptions. The land should be unconditionally donated, or it should be purchased, or not accepted.

The broad and commendable spirit of charity among Methodists caused a great looseness in the management of our churches. Some of our trustees, without consulting their pastor, would let into the church strangers to preach who in many cases had no authority, and who were wicked impostors, and claimed to be independent preachers, and who, once in, would deny our doctrines, deride our government and usages, abuse our men in authority, disparage our ministry, and discourage their support, divide our people, and otherwise seriously damage our cause. The people generally should not countenance *any* preacher who will not give satisfactory evidence of a good Christian and ministerial character. This is an age of fanaticism and impostors. Our preachers should study, and instruct our people in truth and expose all error, discuss living issues. Our people should steadily adhere to their own Church and preachers who come " well recommended." For greater protection our last General Conference enacted a new law. Discipline, Par. 120: " What are the duties of a preacher who has the charge of a circuit, station, or mission? Ans. 1. To preach the gospel, and, in the absence of the presiding elder or bishop, to control the appointment of all services to be held in the churches in his charge." Some, without a knowledge of the needs, think that this law gives too much authority to the pastor; that the trustees, who helped to build the church and who help pay the preacher, ought to have a right to say who should preach in their pulpit. By that rule, why not let the *people* select their preacher? Our itinerancy could not be operated by congregational rules. In that, in the ordinary appointments, our preachers would have to suffer all the evils of the congregational system, and could enjoy none of its advantages. This they would not long submit to. The object of this law was not to give more *authority* to the itinerant preacher who is pastor, but to insure better protection to our people, and also protection to our pastors while they are laboring for us, as any employer must defend his employee. A further principle underlying this law is: When a people build a house of worship, and want the benefit of our Church government and the preaching of our ministry, to get these advantages they must enter a contract with our Church. They, on their part, must deed the property (and it should be untrammeled) to the Methodist Episcopal Church, South, and write in the deed certain specifications; and it is to be subject to the government of said Church. The Church, on its part, agrees to protect the property and give the people the benefit of our government and ministry. Trustees are elected to act for the Church in caring for the property; yet it is all for the practical benefit of the people who built the house and for their successors, any who may become members there, and the entire Methodist Episcopal Church, South, whose property it is. Every other Christian denomination observes the same principles. Some men have such loose ideas of government that they think, as trustees, they have personal ownership in the house and land, and can displace or reject the pastor authoritatively sent them (putting themselves above the Conference, authorities, and laws), and can even lock the church doors against him, and let any other man preach in their house of worship as they may see fit. Such men ought never to be trusted with any office in the Church. They will rend our congregations, and antagonize our faithful preachers, and inveigh against our government, when matters chance to contradict *their* wishes. Let all of our trustees study their official work and obligations, magnify their office, be faithful to God and loyal to the Church, as some of our men already are.

CHAPTER IV.

THE Church cannot afford to put its seal and indorsement upon any man as minister of the gospel simply upon his claim of a divine call to the sacred office, and his request for so important a privilege. The Church must have other evidences that he is "moved by the Holy Ghost to preach."

Discipline, Paragraph 95: "Let the following questions be asked—namely,

" 1. Do they know God as a pardoning God? Have they the love of God abiding in them? Do they desire nothing but God? And are they holy in all manner of conversation?

" 2. Have they gifts (as well as grace) for the work? Have they (in some tolerable degree) a clear, sound understanding, a right judgment in the things of God, a just conception of salvation by faith? Do they speak justly, readily, clearly?

" 3. Have they fruit? Are any truly convinced of sin and converted to God by their preaching?

"As long as these three marks concur in any one, we believe he is called of God to preach."

Discipline, Paragraph 165: " The District Conference shall have authority to license proper persons to preach and to renew their licenses annually, when, in its judgment, their gifts, grace, and usefulness will warrant it."

Paragraph 166: " No person shall be licensed to preach without the recommendation of the Quarterly Conference of the charge to which he belongs; nor shall any one be licensed to preach without first passing, before a committee of three, to be appointed by the presiding elder, an approved examination on the subject of doctrines and discipline, and giving satisfactory evidence of his knowledge of the ordinary branches of an English education."

For many years, as one of the restrictions in licensing men to preach, the following appeared in the Discipline: " Nor shall any one be licensed to preach ... without first being examined, in the Quarterly Conference, on the subject of doctrines and discipline." In 1870 an addition was made to this requirement— viz., " and giving satisfactory evidence of his knowledge of the ordinary branches of an English education."

For a local preacher to be eligible to the office of a deacon, among other requirements, he must pass an approved " examination on the course of study prescribed by the bishops as a preparation for deacon's orders." (See Paragraphs 167, 534.)

For a local deacon to be eligible to the office of an elder, among other requirements, he must pass an approved " examination on the course of study prescribed by the bishops as a preparation for elder's orders." (See Paragraphs 168, 535.)

Now when we have such improved educational facilities, and our people are greatly advancing in intellectual culture, it is necessary for our preachers, local and itinerant, to enjoy at least the advantages of the free-school course. An ignorant man cannot be a wise instructor or a judicious leader, and there are many other emergencies incident to his official position that he cannot meet.

As an addition to Paragraph 166, we need the following: " No member of the Church shall be at liberty to preach without such a license." (See Discipline of the M. E. Church, Paragraph 197.)

By our omission of this specific law, any member of our Church can assume to be a Methodist preacher without distinctly announcing the claim, and thus get the moral, and often the financial, support of the Methodists, when he may not deserve indorsement or recognition of any Church; and we have no means of protection by law. The Church, considering public estimation, could well afford for some laymen to preach without special license, but not for others; yet there could be no distinction. A rule must apply to all alike. This is really the purport of " license," but we allow the lack of specific law abused. We need this regulation to help us form and maintain proper ideas of the importance and sacredness of the Christian ministry and of the Church which allows the license. It is erroneous also to believe that any man, however honorable and righteous, can accomplish more good by being known as an unlicensed preacher. The failure of any man is not due to his having license, but to something else; while his true success should be greatly encouraged by having license. · Rev. R. Abbey wrote: " In what relation does a man stand to the Church or the world, attempting to minister the gospel, who is not personally designated and sent? In proportion as he is intelligent he can but regard himself as an interpolator upon the gospel and an intruder in the sanctuary of the Most High."

Paragraph 169: "It shall be the duty of local preachers to aid the preacher in charge of the circuit, station, or mission to which they belong in supplying the people with the ministry of the word. They shall accordingly be applied to by the preacher in charge, as soon as he enters on his work, to state what amount of service they are able and willing to perform. He may then draw up a plan by which their labors shall be regulated; and they shall be authorized to form new congregations, to take a list of the names of all candidates for Church membership, and, if expedient, receive them into the Church; provided, that all such

congregations, candidates, and members be reported,
as soon as possible, to the preacher in charge, in order
that they may be placed immediately under his pastoral care; and they shall report in writing the extent
and result of their labors to the fourth Quarterly Conference."

The Discipline, pages 77-81, gives other important
directions concerning local preachers; but we have
quoted those parts that specially touch the object of
this writing.

It is a design of the law to so arrange the work,
" wherever it is practicable, as to give the local preachers regular and systematic employment on the Sab-
bath." Sometimes our pastors are embarrassed in the
execution of this provision by the inefficiency and un-
acceptability of a local preacher, yet let us attend to
this duty as far as we can. Many of our local preachers are most acceptable and useful men. Local preachers, through the history of our Church, have held an
honorable position among us, and have been exceedingly useful. We will continue to need them as long
as our ecclesiastical and social conditions remain as
they now are. The local preachers are our reserve
forces for ministerial supply. Besides, they are de-
signed to aid our regular ministry in any " service they
are able and willing to perform." This recognizes
their reserved right to remain at their own home and
engage in secular employment for support; hence no
provision is made for financial remuneration of local
preachers for ministerial work. These reserved rights
are surrendered by our preachers on joining Conference, and in this service of sacrifice they must be pro-
tected and supported before any others. All employ-
ers must protect and support their employees, or their
enterprises will fail, and they will suffer merited dis-
grace. If our people withhold moral and financial

support from the very men who sacrifice most and do most for us and give their support to others, they, that far, become an unfaithful and ungrateful people, and help to dishonor and enfeeble our beloved Church, to which they solemnly promised fidelity of heart and life. If local preachers, from any cause, should be engaged to supply a pastoral charge, they will get pastor's wages. If they do special service in other ways, it is right for the people favored to make proper return; but this should never be allowed by our people to affect in the least the support of their regular ministry. Faithful and loyal local preachers will never knowingly accept any remuneration unjustly turned to them from pastors in charge. Such proceedings would be undermining our itinerancy, upon which our success depends. Neither will an honorable, conscientious local preacher, by his labors or by disparaging remarks or insinuations, hinder the acceptability and success of the appointed pastor.

We require our regular preachers to superintend the preaching to our people; yet some local preachers claim the right to preach where, when, and how they please. Other local preachers antagonize the shepherds of the flocks, and contemn rules to which all our regular preachers must submit; yet they get the support of Methodist influence by being Methodist preachers, thereby forcing our Church to be largely responsible to the public for their conduct as individuals, for their strange doctrines, objectionable methods, and harmful eccentricities. They may count many converts, get handsome remuneration (often part of the pastor's salary), embarrass other Church enterprises, then leave the pastor to mollify irritations, restore the disaffected, pacify the contentious, and harmonize all other discords the best he can. Some of their claims are deceptive—e. g., they claim the right to preach where, when, and as they wish; that they are called to preach, and that they must obey their call, and save as many sinners as possible; that they are impressed by the Holy Spirit to go to certain places and do certain work. A man with such liberty might effect more conversions than if he submitted to the regulations of the Church; but when the undeniable modifiers of such claims are considered, the delusion is clear. He, as an individual, outside of the Church, may urge such claims (he and his God for that); but he has no right to remain in the Church and claim exemption from wise rules that bind others. We cannot allow privileged classes. In such claims a man erects his own impression as sole arbiter, and assumes that no one else should have an impression to resist the arbiter. If any one should dare to resist, he is wicked and fighting against God. In such claims a man also denies that the Church has right to obstruct the execution of his wishes. He may antagonize the regular ministry, abuse the " authorities," deride Church government, scorn " Churchianity," disrupt the Church, and so do far more harm than good; irreparable damage—all this in the Church, just where the devil wants it; but the Church must not interfere. Such men disregard their solemn vows to " support the institutions of the Church"; they are mad, and they should be controlled. No great work, as that of our Church, can be accomplished without organization; and there can be no organization without government, and there can be no government without laws. These laws should be obeyed, and they should be executed. We need union of heart and hand.

We protest against discord and disintegration anywhere and from any source. Rev. R. W. Hood recently wrote: "An alliance of forces is an absolute necessity to the success of our cause. No man can be relied on for good who is too large to subject himself to the powers that be."

These irregularities, with fanatical ideas, were so encouraging looseness and disorganization that the last General Conference found it necessary to protect, in some way, our regular preachers in doing the work we required of them, and protect our people as well, and defend our Church government. The Conference gave us some relief in a specific law, found in Paragraph 120 of the Discipline, in giving the duties of preachers in charge: " To preach the gospel, and, in the absence of the presiding elder or bishop, to control the appointment of all services to be held in the churches in his charge." I fully appreciate the necessity of this law; for its principal occasion seemed to have been in my own charge, in Fulton, Ky., in 1893, when, upon the unauthorized invitation of two of our members there, a disorganizing evangelist, claiming to be a Methodist local preacher, came, and, over the protest of myself and the entire official board, except one of his inviters, held a series of meetings. This conduct was exposed. Our Annual Conference sent to our next General Conference a memorial, which was modified into the law we now have in Paragraph 120. I yet prefer the memorial, though it was not in the best shape; but we have some relief. The purpose of this law is not to require faithful local preachers to get the consent of a pastor every time they preach in one of his churches, but to protect our people and pastors against imposition by placing the authority with him who is held responsible for the spiritual instruction of the people he is appointed to serve. No local preacher who appreciates his honor and his vows and his Church will attempt a violation of this necessary law.

Some local preachers among the people may disparage our regular preachers, depreciate their work, and reduce their support by telling that they themselves are discarded and persecuted by the pastors (which is only in the imagination, of course), and by offering to preach for much less money than the pastor gets, and suggesting that too much authority is given the pastor, and by making other complaints. Many people become disaffected by such talk, and they never note that the local preacher would supplement a small salary by an income from other employments which he has never left to serve the Church; while the itinerant preacher has sacrificed all for the Church, and depends, maybe, solely upon his ministry for support. Besides, they should know that any pastoral charge, to be healthy and strong and to develop in God's service, must sustain a continuous liberality in the support of the Church. Hence, if a local preacher should be appointed to serve a charge as pastor, he should, for the good of the charge and in justice to himself, receive a pastor's wages. No people could depend for a long time upon securing the service of a local preacher, so they must keep in touch and in sympathy with our itinerancy. They should give no countenance to a disloyal local preacher, or any other disorganizer, and they should be alert to discover such.

Our laws are made for the good of all and the hurt of none; and, instead of open or stealthy antagonism to our system, we need cheerful and hearty coöperation on the part of all concerned. In all my charges I have had only one local preacher, whose pastor I was, to treat me or the members unkindly or unfaithfully. The majority of those with whom I have been associated were good and true and useful men in the local ministry. A few of them are even now, as they ought to be, popular as preachers and men among the people with whom they have lived and labored for twenty or thirty years. Let all do as well.

CHAPTER V.

"It is required in stewards, that a man be found faithful." (1 Cor. iv. 2.)

DISCIPLINE, Paragraph 189: " Let the stewards be men of solid piety, who both know and love the Methodist doctrine and discipline, and of good natural and acquired abilities to transact the temporal business of the Church." This describes the character of men suitable for stewards. They should be men of piety, and of solid piety, with no flaws. Then their honesty and religious influence (so much as they may have) can be trusted. Also we cannot afford to put into such a responsible office men who are ignorant of or not in sympathy with our doctrine and discipline. Such men in such position would likely be great hindrances, if they should do us no other hurt. We would be equally hindered by having in this position men incapable of discharging its duties. We should never put men in the office to develop them in any particular. Select, if possible, men, young or old, who already exhibit the qualities prescribed by the Discipline. If the desired number of this kind cannot be had, it would be well to elect to the office only a few, and let them be aided, if necessary, in the execution of their work by some efficient women.

Paragraph 190: " It shall be the duty of the stewards to organize by electing a chairman, secretary, and treasurer; to make estimates of expenses and provision for the support of the gospel; to take an exact account of all the money or other provision collected for the support of the ministry; to make an accurate

(25)

return of every expenditure of money, whether for the
support of the ministry or the relief of the sick or the
poor; to seek the needy and distressed in order to re-
lieve and comfort them; to inform the preachers of any
sick or disorderly persons; to tell the preachers what
they think wrong in them; to attend the official meetings and the quarterly meetings; to give advice, if
asked, in planning the circuit; to attend committees
for the application of money to churches; to give counsel in matters of arbitration; to provide elements for
the Lord's Supper; to appoint some one, whenever necessary, to receive contributions for the support of the
ministry and other purposes, and to obtain from each
collector thus appointed the money received by him,
that it may be reported to the Quarterly Conference;
to take up collections quarterly in every congregation,
if it be necessary, and to write circular letters to the so-
cieties to be more liberal, if need be, as also to let them
know. when occasion requires, the financial state of the
Church, as reported at the Quarterly Conference."

The opinion largely prevails that the work of the
stewards is limited to supervision of the financial support of the preachers; but, according to this quotation
from the Discipline, their sphere is quite comprehensive.   The new board should organize at the time and
place of their election, or as soon thereafter as they can
conveniently do so.   They ought to hold regular meetings for circuit or station; to divide, review, correct,
and, in every way possible, advance their work.   Another work here mentioned is more particularly described in Paragraph 321: " The salary and traveling
expenses of preachers on circuits and stations shall be
estimated by their respective boards of stewards, after
consultation with the preacher in charge."   Every
board of stewards, with right disposition, will obey this
law, and consult their pastor first about his needs for

comfortable support, and learn what he thinks would be right for his salary, and tell him what their people, as they honestly believe, would be able to pay him, then estimate his salary at as large a sum as they can reasonably hope to influence their people to pay. While they appear to have absolute authority by the law to fix the pastor's salary as they ultimately please, they really have no legal or moral right in estimating the preacher's salary to stint him and shirk responsibilities for their people. The law contemplates the stewards acting with great concern and integrity for pastor and people, with as much interest in one as in the other. It is best for both parties that the people pay all they reasonably can.

Paragraph 322: ". . . . Unless otherwise ordered by the Church Conference, the stewards shall adopt the plan of assessment with consent, as provided in the following paragraph (323): . . . The stewards of each station or circuit shall determine whether payments are to be made weekly, monthly, or quarterly during the year. They shall then ascertain how much each member is able and willing to pay in the installments fixed by the stewards. . . ." These duties of stewards measure extraordinary trusts and responsibilities. Do you wonder that the Discipline puts such emphasis upon having suitable men in this office? They are also "to seek the needy and the distressed," to administer to them; to keep well acquainted with the general condition and conduct of the membership, and give the pastor all needed information. If the pastor makes mistakes of any consequence, they are not to rehearse these errors to every willing listener, and thus curtail the pastor's influence, and that far damage the Church, but go directly to him as soon as need be, and give him kind, brotherly counsel. Thus, instead of increasing disaffection,

3

they can easily help to make the preacher a wiser and
more useful man, and add to the concord and prosperity of the Church. Of course they ought to attend
regularly their board and quarterly meetings. They
should let no ordinary interests prevent their faithful
attention to these sacred trusts, with which, in the
providence of God, they have been honored. Then
it is their duty to provide elements for the Lord's Supper whenever this sacrament is to be administered.
The stewards of the congregation where the Quarterly
Conference is held ought always to have the bread and
wine ready, whether their quarterly meeting includes
Sunday or is held only on " a week day." There is
hardly any excuse to justify a failure in this. We
ought, at all proper times, thus to commemorate the
death of our Lord, even if it cost ten times what it does
cost, either in money to purchase the wine or time and
effort to procure it. An omission of this sacred duty
usually indicates a want of love for Christ, a shameful
looseness in management, and sometimes a sinful stinginess. Where the stewards may neglect this duty
the pastors ought, if possible, to see that they attend to
it. Stewards of each congregation should keep a supply of pure (not sour), unfermented grape wine. The
bread should be fresh baked, unleavened cakes, quite
thin and brittle. This bread can be cooked quick be-
tween hot irons of smooth surface—"smoothing irons"
if no better are convenient. "Thou shalt not offer
the blood of my sacrifice with leavened bread." (Ex.
xxiii. 18.)

Certain traits a steward should not have; and if he
has them, he should, by the grace of God, get rid of
them. He should not be selfish, little, stingy, narrow.
"A steward suggested to his pastor that it was in bad
taste for him to buy a beefsteak, seeing that he was dependent upon the charities of his poor flock for a liv-

ing; and suggested that if he (the steward) were in his place he would forego the expensive luxury of coffee." "Let it once be understood that the steward pays but little himself, the effect is like the hot winds of our Western country on vegetation. He may be industrious with others, he is shorn of his strength." "Each member gauges his own contribution by that of the steward's, and failure results." A steward may be narrow and little in estimating his pastor's salary, then he is quite sure to be so in assessing his members. I know of two stewards who belonged to different circuits in different districts, and who, for the most part, acted out the same story, as follows: The circuit had been reduced in number of appointments. Each appointment could by this reduction get more of the time and service of the pastor. At the first stewards' meeting the board insisted that it was right and necessary for each congregation to pay more than they had done. One steward said: "No; I promised my people to see that their assessment should be reduced." They never had even approached what they ought to pay. "If you assess my congregation any more than what I name, I shall see that they do not pay it." Neither man accomplished his demands. Both were enraged; both tried to influence members not to pay quarterage. One rode over the country a great deal to accomplish his purposes. Both persisted in antagonizing their pastors; one succeeded in disaffecting quite a number. Under "complaints" at their next Quarterly Conferences they were dismissed from office, as they should have been; but they continued their "dissension," annoyed the preachers, and in one case increased privation and want in the preacher's family. Of course God will call them to account for these wrongs, yet present damage results from such sinful doings. The pastor and Church suffer. On one of these circuits some of the stewards who advanced the assessment on their own congregation were contracted in their ideas of individual assessment. They assessed a prosperous farmer five dollars, when, as he afterwards told me, he would as readily pay ten. He ought to have paid the ten, notwithstanding the slight assessment. Some stewards will encourage dissatisfaction with some of the lightest assessments. To ask a member, unless extremely poor, to pay less than one dollar for the ministry for the year is educating that member to put a light estimate upon the Church, the ministry, and religion. If a member cannot or will not pay as much as one dollar, let him assume his own responsibility in fixing what he will pay. Sometimes a charge enjoys revivals and large increase of members during the year, and there is still no improvement in the preacher's salary. Frequently circuits are enlarged in number of appointments without any advance in the pastor's salary. The stewards are nearly always the cause of such stagnation. In their course they encourage the new members to value lightly their religion and the Church, and the old members to pay less than the year before, while every member ought to improve each year, if possible. Dr. Clarke said: " Ever try to exceed your former self."

A steward should not be sour, impatient, fault-finding, gloomy, apologetic, timorous. Such a manner often invites refusal and courts failure; such a manner develops in members an idea that the support of their minister is a kind of charity. A faint-hearted steward, apologizing to and for his people, coinciding with them in complaints of " hard times," " no money in the country," " assessed too much," etc., is like the ten dispirited men sent by Moses with Caleb and Joshua to spy out the land of Canaan. They reported that the land was most fruitful, but it was impossible to conquer the numerous and strong people. Caleb and Joshua said: " Let us go up at once, and possess it; for we are well able to overcome it." It was easy to discourage the people, as it is now; so they would have stoned Caleb and Joshua had God not interfered. Those ten men died by the plague. Only Caleb and Joshua and those who were their children were allowed to enter the promised land.

A steward should not be lazy, neglectful, indifferent, or procrastinating. Some men would be offended if they were not continued as stewards; then they must have a list of members to collect from, and they file the list away or lose it, and never collect a dollar till the year is nearly gone, and maybe not then. In continuing such a man in the stewardship the Quarterly Conference becomes accessory to the wrong.

Procrastination is a common and serious fault among stewards. I once visited the Quarterly Conference of a neighboring charge, whose pastor, with his family, suffered much privation. His people were financially strong, but lacked development. A congregation had two stewards, each worth ten or fifteen thousand dollars. One was present. When asked for his report, he said: " Well, Brother J., our other steward, and I have been quite busy. Other interests would call him elsewhere to-day; so we decided to report that we had nothing to report." Preachers could never develop such people with such stewards. That man deserved to be expelled from the Church. Preachers yet dread that circuit.

For the work of the year stewards should certainly begin well. The members should pay their dues regularly (and the oftener the better), without being asked for it; yet the stewards should visit every delinquent member at stated times, and, if possible, secure a settlement of a proportional part of the assessment of each one. Doubtless there are members on many charges who have not for five years been asked for quarterage.

I am convinced that most failures on the part of the Church to meet her financial obligations to her ministers are induced by some imperfection, voluntary or otherwise, on the part of the stewards. " Like priest, like people," is true; like steward, like people, is equally true. Oliver Cromwell is quoted as saying: " Not only strike while the iron is hot, but make it hot by striking." Church finances should be operated by this rule.

A steward should be liberal himself, not ashamed for any one to know what he pays. A liberal man, chairman of a board of stewards, told me that he could never learn what two of his stewards paid to the Church. He doubted any payments at all.

A steward ought to love and study his work, and study his members, and learn to manage them wisely. His heart should be burdened with a sense of his duties. He should be broad-minded, progressive, energetic, heroic, cheerful, and hopeful; wise, prompt, patient, but persistent. He may meet with cold repulses and meet people disgusting with their excuses, but such persons most need his best efforts. He should be watchful, timely; ready to persuade, convince, instruct. He should have ready for use verses of the Bible. They must surrender the Bible and their claims to being Christians, or give. He should remind slothful members of their vows of Church membership " to support the institutions of the Church," and explain that these vows are just such as they made to God when, as penitents, they consecrated their lives to his service. They cannot get rid of these obligations, wheresoever they may go; and if they love God and his cause, they have no desire to be rid of them.

Some ignorant men persuaded some of our gullible members to withdraw from our Church and unite with them in a nonprogressive organization, where they would have but little to do, and with that acknowledged purpose. There was no occasion for them to flee from the burden they carried in our Church. Then for designing men to lead them into another communion to do still less for God's cause, to suffer many disadvantages, and to have very few of the advantages before enjoyed, is exceedingly unfortunate for the victims of such practice. In accomplishing disturbances of this sort, the seducers so exhibit the old Adam that is in them that it is strange their own people do not spurn them. God wants his children to " bear more fruit." The Bible also declares: " He which soweth sparingly shall reap also sparingly; and he which soweth bountifully shall reap also bountifully." These erratics teach and encourage the people to thus disregard God's will, deny the Bible, and slight their own best interests for time and eternity. Our stewards, if posted as they should be, can help make firm our unstable members and friends, that they " be no more children, tossed to and fro, and carried about with every wind of doctrine by the sleight of men and cunning craftiness, whereby they lie in wait to deceive."

In Quarterly Conference I asked an efficient steward on a circuit to tell us how he succeeded so well. He replied, in substance: " Our people pay quarterly. In sufficient time I request my members to bring me their quarterage by a certain day, nearly a week before Quarterly Conference. On the appointed day I visit all my delinquent members for quarterage. Before starting, in secret prayer I ask God to prepare me and my people to do our duty. Often I pray with them in their homes."

Another successful steward said: " I will begin now and work till the next Quarterly Conference. I see every member several times. I suit my appeals to the disposition and conditions of each member."

Another one said: " I encourage my members to lay by, as they have opportunities, money to pay Church dues. So they generally have it ready. I also urge that every member should pay something. Two very poor sisters, who plow and do other such work for an honorable living, wanted to pay each twenty-five cents for the ministry, but had no money. I paid it for them. Within reasonable time they paid me."

One of our preachers related to me an experience of his, in substance, as follows: " I was a local preacher in —— Circuit, with my membership at ——, where we had only thirty-five poor members, with a log schoolhouse to worship in. I was made steward. At the first Quarterly Conference I was asked what my congregation would pay that year for the ministry. I answered: ' Fifty dollars.' Other stewards present were astonished. They urged that my members were poor; that they had never been assessed over fifteen dollars; that they seldom paid that; and that, with fifty dollars imposed upon them, they would not pay anything. I urged that they had never been taught right; that they were not too poor to pay fifty dollars; that they ought to pay it, and would do so. While I ought not to put too heavy burdens on my members, I ought not to shirk for them what was their real duty. After much contention, I was allowed to try the fifty dollars. I distributed that sum among all the members, including the children; so that each one had but little to pay. I immediately saw them, and told them what had occurred and what I thought. Without hesitation, every one promised his assessment, and to

bring me the money soon. It was all paid within six
months."

A northern brother moved to one of our towns and
joined our Church. Everybody there loved the Methodist preacher; but the stewards reported one hundred
dollars behind, and that they could do no more. The
new man, who had been there several months, said:
" It must be paid. One of you go with me to-day,
and another go with me to-morrow, and we will try."
After this effort, he called together the stewards,
locked the door, and said: " Brethren, we lack thirty
dollars yet, but it must be paid. I have already paid
more than my assessment, and there is five dollars
more. Mr. A., cover that with a five." It was done.
He appealed to each one. Some hesitated long and
offered many excuses; but he would accept none, and
would contend that this obligation should be met. It
was accomplished. The pastor and the Church rejoiced together. Doubtless that northern brother's
spirit has had much influence in the development of
that Church and its present prosperity.

We need more system in our Church finances. We
have in some districts congregations of one hundred
and seventy-five to two hundred members who are usually assessed from fifty to seventy-five dollars, and
they seldom pay their assessment. In such cases, as
a rule, their stewards do not, and maybe cannot, lead
them right. They have no financial system. In a
few cases the stewards do not even divide among themselves the list of members for collection. A short
time, usually about a day, before the Quarterly Conference, and often the very morning of the Quarterly
Conference, they go out for money. Some members
may be called upon by several stewards, prompt members; but one hundred and fifty or more may not be
visited by any steward. Then the preacher and his

family suffer want, which necessarily weakens the ar-
dor of the preacher in his work; and all those neglected
members remain undeveloped and unuseful, and the
cause of God languishes—all the result of the unbusi-
nesslike methods of the leaders.

The Discipline does not specify that our stewards
are to hunt our people for these funds; it is expected
that all contributors carry their money to those authorized to receive it; yet if this is not done regularly
enough, the stewards ought, as is our custom, to visit
those in arrears. (Read Ex. xxxvi. 1-7.) The Israelites brought contributions, " free offerings," " for the
work of the service of the sanctuary," until, by com-
mandment of Moses, " the people were restrained from
bringing "; for they had more than " sufficient."
That was thirty-four hundred years ago, yet many of
our people now are not up with those Israelites.

The assessment plan, and payments to be made
weekly or monthly or quarterly, is proved to be the
best.   The more frequent the payments, the better for
all concerned, and the more surely will obligations be
met.   Each collecting steward ought to keep a collection book, in which should be kept, neatly and correctly written, accounts with members, preachers, and
the treasurer, and his own Quarterly Conference reports, as suggested by the plan of Brother T. N.
Wilkes, one of the pastors of Paris District.   His
stewards' Quarterly Conference reports consisted of
about five questions and answers, which revealed the
work of the steward; and it had a most wholesome effect.   Using this suggestion, we incorporated a more
comprehensive blank report in a " Steward's Collection Book," recently devised, and which, we hope, will
accomplish good.   A steward's collection book should
always be ready for inspection by any member of our
Church.   In the order of business for the Quarterly

Conference, prescribed in the Discipline, we need the following question to appear just after the eighteenth "inquiry": "Have the stewards 'Steward's Collection Books,' and have they kept them correctly?" (The Conference shall call for these books to be examined.) [1 and 4.]

RECORDING STEWARD.

The Discipline, Paragraph 195, thus defines the duties of a recording steward: "To preserve the records of the Quarterly Conference, and to report to the Joint Board of Finance of the Annual Conference a full account of the acts of his board of stewards the preceding year, and to have the same at the Quarterly Conference and at the District Conference for examination." He should not be negligent or careless, but faithful in all these duties. Bishop McTyeire, in "Manual of the Discipline," page 252, furnishes the following form for report of recording steward:

To the Joint Board of Finance of the ——— Annual Conference of the Methodist Episcopal Church, South, to be held at ———, December 8, 187—.

Dear Brethren: The undersigned Recording Steward of ——— Circuit (Station or Mission), of ——— District, of ——— Annual Conference, submits the following report of the acts of the Board of Stewards of said circuit (station or mission) for the year ending December 8, 187—.

Estimated for preacher in charge	$1,000 00
Paid	900 00
Estimated for presiding elder	100 00
Paid	90 00
Estimated for bishops	10 00
Paid	8 00
Estimated for Conference collections	140 00
Paid	150 00

G. W. W——, R. S.

SALEM, S. C., *November* 20, 187—.

DISTRICT STEWARDS.

The Discipline, Paragraph 85, directs the Quarterly Conference to elect stewards, " and of the stewards to appoint one a recording and one a district steward."

Paragraph 196 directs: " There shall be held annually, in every district, a meeting composed of one steward from each pastoral charge, to be elected by the Quarterly Conference, on the nomination of the presiding elder, at the annual election of stewards. It shall be their duty, after consultation with the presiding elder, who shall preside in such meeting, to estimate the traveling expenses and salary of the presiding elder, and apportion the same, together with the collections ordered by the Annual Conference and apportioned to said district by the Joint Board of Finance, among the several charges of the district, according to their ability."

It is exceedingly important that each district steward should attend this meeting and represent his own charge. Sometimes in the absence of a steward his pastor is recognized as the representative. This is not legal, and it should not be encouraged; yet it may sometimes become expedient. When a steward is in attendance, his pastor, if present, should be reticent, except when questioned, or it becomes necessary for him to offer information that will not be known otherwise; then he should delicately and briefly make his statement. I have known of only one instance of a preacher acting indiscreetly; yet hindrances of this sort have been such that the district stewards, by resolution, refused the attendance of all who could not legally be present.

District stewards should appreciate the office of presiding elder, and realize that it is indispensable to the Methodist itinerancy. His salary should accord with his needs and his work. His expenses are necessarily heavy, and the perquisites of his office are very small. His work is heavier probably than that of any two of the pastors. As a rule, our presiding elders have qualifications that would claim for them good salaries in the pastorate; and our districts cannot afford, by sorry support, to force the appointment of only inefficient men to this office. For the benefit of pastors and people we need as presiding elders most efficient men to encourage development in all interests. His salary should be divided among the charges according to salaries of pastors, which should express their ability and willingness to pay to the support of the ministry.

CHAPTER VI.

FINANCIAL SUPPORT OF THE CHURCH.

IN treating this important subject, I fear that an effort at *multum in parvo* may cause me to be blunt at times; but I will try to avoid the several errors that now threaten me.

Certainly all of us have faults; possibly all of us have merits. We should cherish our excellences and correct our defects. To be wise, then, we should not decline to look upon our own mistakes, though disagreeable. The Bible specially may be a mirror to us to help our adorning.

Among Christians and the irreligious, one of the most extensive sins is avaricious covetousness. It is seductive and destructive to an individual, and obstructive to the Church. God, in his Book, condemns this sin and warns us of its evils.

In the study of words, some think Cain's sin " was withholding what was God's." Deut. v. 21: " Neither shalt thou desire thy neighbor's wife, neither shalt thou covet thy neighbor's house, his field, . . . his ox, or his ass, or anything that is thy neighbor's." Ps. x. 3: " For the wicked boasteth of his heart's desire, and blesseth the covetous, whom the Lord abhorreth." Luke xii. 15: "And he said unto them, Take heed, and beware of covetousness: for a man's life consisteth not in the abundance of the things which he possesseth." Isa. v. 8: " Woe unto them that join house to house, that lay field to field, till there be no place, that they may be placed alone in the midst of the earth! " (See also verses 9, 10.) Isa. lvii. 17: "For the iniquity of his covetousness was I wroth, and smote

(40)

him: I hid me, and was wroth, and he went on frowardly in the way of his heart." Deut. viii. 11-17: "Beware . . . lest when thou hast eaten and art full, and hast built goodly houses, and dwelt therein; and when thy herds and thy flocks multiply, and thy silver and thy gold is multiplied, and all that thou hast is multiplied; then thine heart be lifted up, and thou forget the Lord thy God. . . . And thou say in thine heart, My power and the might of my hand hath gotten me this wealth." 1 Tim. vi. 9, 10: "But they that will be rich fall into temptation and a snare, and into many foolish and hurtful lusts, which drown men in destruction and perdition. For the love of money is the root of all evil: which while some coveted after, they have erred from the faith, and pierced themselves through with many sorrows." Mark x. 25: "It is easier for a camel to go through the eye of a needle, than for a rich man to enter into the kingdom of God." Christ teaches that it is impossible for a man who puts his heart on riches instead of God to enter his kingdom. In Luke xii. 16-21 Christ represents a rich man who decided to build larger barns and store away his goods for many years, then to take his ease, eat, drink, and be merry, rather than to lay up treasures in heaven. "But God said unto him, Thou fool, this night thy soul shall be required of thee: then whose shall those things be, which thou hast provided? So is he that layeth up treasure for himself, and is not rich toward God." Such a man is an idolater. Col. iii. 5: "Covetousness, which is idolatry." Eph. v. 5: "Nor covetous man, who is an idolater, hath any inheritance in the kingdom of Christ and of God." Such a man has more confidence in the power of his money than in the power and love and fidelity of God. It is not that there is sin in a gold or silver dollar or any number of

them, any more than in any other metal; but the sin
is in putting one's heart and trust in these perishable
things, rather than in the worship and services and
providence of God.

A beautiful lesson appears in Matt. vi. 19-34. Is
your life annoyed with consuming care for something
to eat? " Behold the fowls of the air: for they sow
not, neither do they reap, nor gather into barns; yet
your heavenly Father feedeth them. Are ye not
much better than they? " Are you making life a burden to yourself in an effort for raiment? " Consider
the lilies of the field, how they grow; they toil not,
neither do they spin: and yet I say unto you, That even
Solomon in all his glory was not arrayed like one of
these. Wherefore, if God so clothe the grass of the
field, . . .   shall he not much more clothe you,
O ye of little faith? . . .   Seek ye first the kingdom of God, and his righteousness; and all these things
shall be added unto you." This duty claims prece-
dence in time and importance. If the Bible be true,
the reward promised justifies obedience. This pas-
sage does not encourage us in indolence, or expecta-
tion that God will feed us in the same way he does
birds, or clothe us in the same way he does flowers. If
we seek and enjoy the kingdom of God and his righteousness, we will be industrious; yet we can have
sweet rest in him, knowing that he will as certainly
provide for us, after our kind, as he does for the birds
and lilies each after their kind. Here is a " Christian's secret of a happy life." To seek satisfaction
in worldly wealth is like pursuing a mirage: it is eva-
sive. Prov. xxiii. 4, 5: " Labor not to be rich. . . .
Wilt thou set thine eyes upon that which is not? for
riches certainly make themselves wings; they fly away
as an eagle toward heaven." Isa. lv. 2: " Wherefore do ye spend money for that which is not bread?

and your labor for that which satisfieth not? hearken diligently unto me, and eat ye that which is good, and let your soul delight itself in fatness." In Prov. xxx. 8, Agur was wise: "Give me neither poverty nor riches; feed me with food convenient for me." James i. 11: "The sun is no sooner risen with a burning heat, but it withereth the grass, and the flower thereof falleth, and the grace of the fashion of it perisheth: so also shall the rich man fade away in his ways." But "the word of the Lord endureth forever"; and if we obey it, we shall live forever. It teaches that what we may have, much or little, came by God's blessings upon our labors. (Deut. viii. 18.) 1 Cor. iv. 7: "What hast thou that thou didst not receive? now if thou didst receive it, why dost thou glory, as if thou hadst not received it?" (See also 1 Kings xx. 3; Ps. l. 10-12.) We should not waste our substance, whatever it be, in riotous living, but "gladly spend and be spent" in God's service; for we are his. Rom. xiv. 8: "Whether we live, we live unto the Lord; and whether we die, we die unto the Lord: whether we live therefore, or die, we are the Lord's." 1 John iii. 17, 18: "Whoso hath this world's goods, and seeth his brother have need, and shutteth up his bowels of compassion from him, how dwelleth the love of God in him? . . . Let us not love in word, neither in tongue; but in deed and in truth." Many show very little love for God by deeds of charity or direct support of the Church, at home or abroad; yet the Bible is abundant in teachings upon these obligations. Eph. ii. 10: "We are his workmanship, created in Christ Jesus unto good works," etc. This verse and its context and parallel passages teach that it is not by good works we are brought into Christ, but by the "washing of regeneration, and renewing of the Holy Ghost"—his workmanship. In this production there is then fixed an

4

element, or principle, of interest in and love for God and his cause that will express itself in results: "*Created* in Christ Jesus *unto good* works." " Faith, if it hath not works, is dead."

One of our members owns over a thousand acres of valuable land, much fine stock, money drawing interest, and every year sells several hundred dollars' worth of tobacco, and other produce as well; and he pays ("*gives*") one dollar to the Church. In another community lives a member who owns several hundred acres of land, and does nearly as well as the first mentioned, in worldly prosperity; yet he pays ("*gives*") twenty-five cents annually for the gospel. A lady of the Church asked him if this report of the stewards was true. He replied: " Of course; I am not able to pay any more." She rejoined: " That is all the religion you get, twenty-five cents' worth." He never had that. True religion, in large enough field, will yield more fruit than that in any soil. We have still another member, who owns three farms, has the finest stock within ten miles of him, lends money at big interest, makes money generally. The steward, his neighbor, is poor, lives on a rented farm, but pays eight dollars a year. He replied to the steward: "An *assessment* of five dollars! I'll never pay it!" " Will you pay $2.50, then?" " No; I can stay at home cheaper than that, and I'll do it." That unfortunate congregation had another member nearly as bad. They might do well to outwit the devil by expelling those men from the Church.

One of our stewards said in Quarterly Conference: " I have on my list names of some hard cases. One man has a good home, has enough of everything needful; but he has paid to the Church only $2.50 in the last seventeen years." Another steward, on a different circuit, said: " I have on my list the name of a man who sells every year six or seven thousand pounds of cotton, other things as well, holds prayer meetings, talks in revivals, exhorts, and shouts, and pays the Church each year one dollar for himself, wife, and two children, and will not pay more."

In pastoral charge of a certain station, Mrs. Wilson and I were improving the churchyard, which work had been needed for many years. I went to a merchant, a member of our Church, for a small wooden box (6x10x5 inches) in which to plant a geranium for the churchyard. He charged me ten cents for it. Another merchant, a steward, charged me five cents for a five-cent ball of twine to be used with vines. Each man knew the object of my purchase. I probably never, even now, see either of those men without feeling an impulse of pity that he, an intelligent human being, from a selfish, narrow, blind, covetous spirit, should become so insensible to Christian and civil proprieties. Many preachers have had such experiences, yet such men are comparatively few; so they make an impression when we do endure their touch.

In another charge was a member of our Church, "Uncle Ab. Akers," who loved his Church, and was glad to do anything he possibly could for it, though he was quite a poor man. The stewards assessed him a small sum. He said to them: "That is not enough; I will pay ten dollars." He paid it. Sometimes he would work two or three days improving the parsonage or its premises, and would never accept from me any pay, unless it was work the Church engaged him to do; and then it was quite a moderate charge, if any at all. I paid him only by giving him presents. When I would be from home, in passing the parsonage he would stop every day and ask Mrs. Wilson if he could do anything for her, and would say: "I must see after my preacher's family when he is from home." He died suddenly;

and certainly no community ever sorrowed over the
death of any citizen more than that town and its community, white and black, did over his death. Even
his dog, for three weeks or more after his burial, would
lie upon his grave, and only leave his watch to go for
his meals, and return. The people erected a modest
monument to that man's memory; and I now gladly,
yet sadly, make this record of that good man.

We have providentially distributed over the district many good and true members, who, I trust, will
serve as leaven to affect for good the whole body; yet
we have many men and women such as described
above. They remind me of a letter from Silas Gan-
derfoot, of Ciderville Circuit, to his "Deer Jess."
The new preacher, "Bruther Sunshine," in his sermons was pressing subscriptions for the new "meetin'
house." Silas wrote: "I kan't tell you how quick I
got nervous when he begun to tawk like that, fur I
didcnt kno what minit he wud spile the meetin' by
goin' in at it and takin' up a kulluckshun. I like to
set under preechen ez well ez anybody, so long ez it
hain't nuthin' more than preechen; but Ide ruther bo
'most anywhere else than in a meetin' house when a
preecher stops iggszortin' and goes to beggin'. Unkel
Peelez and Bruther Kalup Chiller and me has ben kep
on a strane ever sense the noshun was fust started of
buildin' a new meetin' house, and there hain't no tell-
in' what may happen to us before it's up and paid fur.
Unkel Peelez sez he has the mizry in his chist so mutch
now that mebbe he ort to go and visit fur a few munths
with his dawter up in Mishigin. Frum the way he
tawks Ike 'spect about the only thing that will keep
him from doin' it is the turrible price they charge fur
travelin' on the railroads. I tell you, Jess, it's a-git-
tin' to be a dredful site harder to injoy religyun thun
it was when Bruther Skybuster was a-livin' in the pas-

sunidge. It seems to me that it's a shame that folks who think ez mutch ov munny ez I do shud be kep in sech konstant danger ov having to part with it. I don't mind doin' my part tords the preecher by takin' a basket ov stuff now and then to the passunidge; but when it kums to shellin' out greenbax, I don't keer what you say, it makes me feel ez tho' I don't keer mutch if I do backslide. I like to set purty well tords the frunt in meetin', and never feel sorry that I've jined church when Ime at a funeral; but when Ime tormented until I jest hav to put my hand in my pocket and give away so mutch kold munny, it takes the courage out uv me so kumplete that I don't feel ez tho' I had a bit more backbone than a yarn gallus."

All such people who are able, but will not do, ought to bring themselves into judgment, as a Brother Hastin, of Manlyville Circuit, did five years ago. He questioned: " If I had a man serving me as I serve the Lord, what would I do with him? I would not pay him, and I would dismiss him." There in the woods he knelt in prayer. Since then he has been trying to do his duty. God blesses us in duty, not out of it.

The New York *Observer* furnished the following story, with its good lesson: "At a meeting of leading members of three city churches, called to raise money for an important new enterprise, there was little response in the way of subscription, though all applauded the object. Dr. Brainard (for thirty years a pastor in Philadelphia) arose, faced the rich men, and thus addressed them: ' Brethren, the Lord has denied to you the privilege of exercising many of the most precious graces of the Christian character which, in his infinite mercy, he has vouchsafed to the rest of us. You never knew what it was to repose absolute, unassisted faith in God for the things of this world; you never had to go to sleep at night without knowing where your breakfast was to come from; you never had a sick child wasting away for the want of costly luxuries; you never had to deny yourself the gratification of the impulses of pity when a sufferer came to your door; you never had to endure the humiliation of being dunned for an honest debt without knowing whether you could ever pay it. All these unspeakable advantages in developing Christian character inscrutable Providence has taken from you and bestowed upon us poor men. The one solitary grace of the Christian life which has been denied to us and given to you is the grace of liberality; and if you don't exercise that, the Lord have mercy on your souls.' That bold appeal did the work." Many of our people of moderate means also need Dr. Brainard's exhortation.

Rev. J. H. Pritchett wrote in *Review of Missions:* " By every available token we are justified in measuring the genuineness and depth of a member's spiritual life by the generosity of his giving. Think as you may, talk and write as you please, it is nevertheless unquestionably true that a man's profession of religion can be better tested and measured by the motive and extent of his giving than by any other known method."

The Bible gives much instruction on our obligation to the poor, and many such passages are most encouraging with precious promises to the obedient and charitable and liberal: " He that hath a bountiful eye shall be blessed; for he giveth of his bread to the poor." " He hath dispersed, he hath given to the poor; his righteousness endureth forever; his horn shall be exalted with honor." " If thou draw out thy soul to the hungry, and satisfy the afflicted soul; then shall thy light rise in obscurity, and thy darkness be as the noonday. And the Lord shall guide thee contin-

ually, and satisfy thy soul in drought, and make fat
thy bones: and thou shalt be like a watered garden,
and like a spring of water, whose waters fail not."
" He that hath pity upon the poor lendeth unto the
Lord; and that which he hath given will he pay him
again."   " He that giveth to the poor shall not lack."
" Cast thy bread upon the waters; for thou shalt find
it after many days."   " Give, and it shall be given
unto you; good measure, pressed down, and shaken together, and running over, shall men give into your
bosom."   " Charge them that are rich in this world,
. . . that they be rich in good works, ready to dis-
tribute, willing to communicate; laying up in store for
themselves a good foundation against the time to come,
that they may lay hold on eternal life."   " Honor the
Lord with thy substance, and with the first fruits of all
thine increase: so shall thy barns be filled with plenty,
and thy presses shall burst out with new wine."   So
God justly demands the "*first fruits*"—not the last
and superfluous or unmarketable—from flocks, herds,
or fields.   God said (Ex. xx.): " I am the Lord thy
God, which have brought thee out of the land of
Egypt, out of the house of bondage."   Suggestive.
Then follows the first of the Ten Commandments:
" Thou shalt have no other gods before me. . . ;
For I the Lord thy God am a jealous God."   *All* our
good comes from him, even our very life.   He has the
highest claim upon us.   We should form no debts we
cannot pay; but, of all obligations, allow none to su-
persede God's claim.   One of our stewards, a good
man, but in error, still owed some for his productive
farm and enjoyable home, the payment of which he
could more wisely defer than to repudiate part of his
assessment for the Church, which was already too
small.   He withheld his crop of tobacco from market
to get a better price.   He began his economy with the

Church, where many others begin, while obligations to God and his Church should be the first met. It is true, a man is not, by legal process, forced to pay this; besides, if he omits this indebtedness till after Conference, it, as a debt, is canceled. As mere means of escape these avenues should never be traveled by any one. Honorable principle should be as binding as any civil or ecclesiastical law. Thus many put God's claims last, and do not allow them on a basis even of equal importance with others, while they should be first. " The first of the first fruits of thy land thou shalt bring into the house of the Lord thy God." " Likewise shalt thou do with thine oxen, and with thy sheep." Paul classed the grace of liberality with that of faith, etc. 2 Cor. viii. 7, 8: " Therefore, as ye abound in everything, in faith, and utterance, and knowledge, and in all diligence, and in your love to us, see that ye abound in this grace also, . . . to prove the sincerity of your love." God is well pleased with such exhibitions of love. Cornelius saw in a vision coming unto him an angel of God, who said: " Thy prayers and thine alms are come up for a memorial before God." " But to do good and to communicate forget not: for with such sacrifices God is well pleased."

For the maintenance of the Levites, whom God chose for the service of his tabernacle and temple, the Jews were commanded to appropriate the tenth part of the produce of their fields; also the tenth of their goats, sheep, and horned cattle. (Num. xviii. 21; Lev. xxvii. 32.) Another division of a tenth was applied in the temple service for the celebration of certain feasts. Special provisions were also made for the poor. All this was, as God said, " that thou mayest learn to fear the Lord thy God always." It succeeded also in the cultivation of a beneficent spirit, most worthy, which was often exhibited in *voluntary contributions*. For building the tabernacle in the wilderness God, through Moses, said to them (Ex. xxxv. 5): " Whosoever is of a *willing heart*, let him bring . . . an offering of the Lord; gold, and silver, and brass," etc. Verse 21: "And they came, every one whose heart stirred him up, and every one whom his spirit made *willing*. . . . They came, both men and women, as many as were *willing-hearted*, and brought bracelets, and earrings, . . . all jewels of gold," etc., choicest of their possessions. With " *willing hearts* " they contributed more than enough, and Moses restrained them. Six hundred years pass by. "Athaliah, that wicked woman, had broken up the house of God; and also all the dedicated things of the house of the Lord did they bestow upon Baalim." Joash came to the throne, and " was minded to repair the house of the Lord." They put a chest " without the gate of the house of the Lord. . . . All the people rejoiced, and brought in, and cast into the chest, until they had made an end, . . . and gathered money in abundance." Their system and education, in spite of their occasional lapses into idolatry, induced those people to be liberal and to *bring their contributions to the temple*. Besides, " it was a constant custom for all who entered the temple to carry money with them to give to the treasury or to the poor or to both." (Clarke on Acts iii. 5.) Our people—men, women, and children—should practice the same customs. The reflex influence of our financial support of the Church, at home and abroad, is like to that of other parts of worship, song, prayer, meditation, hearing a sermon. In proper mind, a people would not have their religious fervor repressed by an appropriate collection, but enhanced. Sam Jones said: " No meeting is what it ought to be till the sis-

ters can shout all the way through a collection." In
such practice we expel selfishness and learn sympathy
for humanity. "It is more blessed to give than to receive." "No man can be a Christian and consume
God's bounty upon himself." This lesson is impres-
sive as it appears in Matt. xx. 20-29. The world
would estimate an individual by his position, attained
one way or another. Christ presents a different ideal:
"Whosoever will be great among you, let him be your
minister; and whosoever will be chief among you, let
him be your servant: even as the Son of man came not
to be ministered unto, but to minister, and to give his
life a ransom for many."

Some think they are too poor to pay or give anything. J. H. Pritchett again wrote: "Every re-
deemed soul has something wherewith to pay and give,
as unto the Lord; if not dollars, then cents; if not
cents, then some other testimonial of obligation and
gratitude, work, prayer, praise—something, ' according to that he hath, not according to that he hath not.'
The two turtledoves, or the two young pigeons, in
the hands of honest poverty were equally valuable in
God's esteem with the lamb, or even the bullock, in
the hands of the rich." We are ready to labor and
make sacrifice for any object of our affections. If we
love God and his Church and have faith in his care for
us, we are ready and *anxious* to make any sacrifice we
reasonably can in his service. (Mark xii. 41-44.)
Christ saw many that were rich cast much into the
treasury. A poor widow "threw in two mites, which
make a farthing"—half a cent of our money. Christ
said: "This poor widow hath cast more in than all
they which have cast into the treasury; for all they did
cast in of their abundance; but she of her want did
cast in all that she had, even all her living." She
proved the sincerity of her love and faith also.

Dr. Kelley is quoted as saying: "No one who has been a member of the Church twelve months without paying something to its support has any right to call himself or herself a Christian." He is likely correct. I said: "Any one not dependent on the Church for aid is able to help the Church." A Brother Shelton, a minister of another Church, modified my views somewhat by relating the following: "My congregation put into my hands five dollars and requested me to carry it to old Brother Jones, who had long been sick at his little home. He was very poor, needed medicine and more suitable diet. The old soldier for a while held the money in his hand and wept. Then, with messages of love to his benefactors, he returned one dollar, saying: 'Give this to the Church as my contribution for its work.'"

Near Hollow Rock Junction lives, with her children, a good woman, about ninety years old, and quite poor in this world's goods. Every year she dried fruit, picked cotton, and did other work for money to pay two dollars to her pastor, Brother Fuzzell. She made monthly payments. She would not accept this money from her children. One year she planted beans, cultivated, gathered, and sold them for money with which she bought calico to use in making a quilt for a present to her pastor's wife. She alone made the quilt. I enjoyed the privilege of sleeping one night under that quilt. I felt unusually safe under such a covering. Do you discover any superstition in that last sentence? That may be a window through which you may look in; I do not know.

The *Pacific Methodist* gave the following: "A pastor one day visited one of his parishioners, a poor woman, who lived in one small room, and made a living by her needle. He says: 'She put three dollars into my hand and said, "There is my contribution to the

Church fund." "But you are not able to give so
much." "O, yes," she replied, "I have learned how
to give now." "How is that?" I asked. "Three
months ago you preached a sermon in which you told
us that you did not believe one of your people was so
poor but that if he loved Christ he could find some
way of showing that love by his gifts. I went home
and had a good cry over that sermon. I said to myself, ' My minister don't know how poor I am, or he
never could have said that'; but from crying I at last
got to praying, and when I told Jesus all about it, I
seemed to get an answer in my heart that dried up all
tears." "What was the answer?" I asked, deeply
moved by her recital. "Only this, ' If you cannot
give as other people do, give like a little child'; and I
have been doing it ever since. When I have a penny
over from my sugar or loaf of bread, I lay it aside for
Jesus; and so I have gathered it all in pennies. Since
I began to give to the Lord, I have always had more
money in the house for myself; and it is wonderful
how the work comes pouring in. So many are coming to see me that I never knew before. It used to
be I could not pay my rent without borrowing something, but it is so no more. The dear Lord is so kind."
This poor woman in five months brought fifteen dollars, all saved in a nice little box I had given her; and
in twelve months twenty-one dollars. She apparently
grew more in Christian character in that one year than
in all the previous years of her connection with the
Church.' "

The *Union Gospel News* gave the following incident of Mr. Kincaid's work in 1841, as he recorded it
of " Karen Woman's Rupee: " " ' I went to the house ·
of an aged woman who worshiped God. For several
months she had been unable to leave the house, and
was fast wearing out with consumption. She has

four children; but one is blind, and another is deaf. She is very poor. The house might have been worth fifteen rupees, and all in it fifteen more [an East Indian coin; " the current silver rupee is valued at forty-six cents "]. She could talk but little on account of her cough, but expressed great anxiety for the eternal welfare of her children. After about an hour spent in conversation and prayer, I rose to take my leave, when the poor woman bade me remain a little longer. She crept along to another part of the house; and, returning soon, she put into my hand a rupee. I could not comprehend what she meant, and said: " What is to be done with this? " " This is very little," she replied; " but it is all I have, and it is to help the cause of Christ." " But you are old and infirm and poor." " Yes; but I love Christ, and this is very little." Surely, I thought, here in the midst of poverty and decrepitude is a converted heathen exercising the enlightened faith which works by love, purifies the heart, and overcomes the world. For days I could not cease from reflecting on the expression, " This is to help the cause of Christ "; and when I thought of the withered hand and wrinkled face of her who gave it, that rupee was magnified to a thousand times its real value.' "

Miss Ida M. Worth visited in Japan the famous temple called Kompira San, where thousands of pilgrims go every year to worship. She found many pilgrims on the steps worshiping. She said: " They always paid their money first, clapped their hands, and then made their prayer."

The pastor of a negro congregation near Manlyville, Tenn., two and a half years ago told Brother N. R. Waters that his twenty-one members there promised him forty dollars; that they paid him monthly, and that they never failed to pay what they promised.

In the southern part of the district is another negro

congregation, which numbered sixty members, and which promised their pastor eighty dollars, and never thought of failure. Every one paid something, and they paid monthly. Many other negro congregations are doing as well, for which we should all be thankful to God. Of course many do nothing, or but little.

Some of our own congregations, specially the stations and a few in the country, deserve much credit for their fidelity, while others never do so well. Last year there were eighteen pastoral charges in the district. Eleven of them assessed for the support of their preacher less than one dollar per member. In some of our congregations one-third of the members, in others one-half, in others two-thirds, and in some others four-fifths of the members pay nothing at all for the support of the ministry; and these same persons seldom pay anything for any interest in the Church.

Several years ago an Irish woman entered our car as we passed Bartlett, going to Memphis. The conductor soon called for her ticket. In a *very* brusk manner she said: "No, sir; I have no ticket." "Then please pay the money," he said. "I have no money. You shall carry me into the city free." "I cannot so violate the rules of the road," he responded. "You *shall*, sir," she declared. He reached for the bell rope to stop the train to put her off, but she then said: "Here! If you are going to do that way, I'll pay you." She opened her purse and paid him full fare. I thought: How many are trying thus to "beat their way" to the "heavenly Jerusalem," but the rules of the road forbid!

Paul, in 2 Cor. viii. 2-5, writes of the liberality of the poor churches of Macedonia: "How that in a great trial of affliction the abundance of their joy and their deep poverty abounded unto the riches of their liberality. . . . Beyond their power they were

willing of themselves.   . . . And this they did,
not as we hoped, but first gave their own selves to the
Lord." Their liberality was an easy consequence of
their gift of themselves to the Lord.   Paul, by " occasion of the forwardness of others," exhorts the Corinthians " to prove the sincerity of their love," and
argues also the example of the sacrifice of Christ:
" For ye know the grace of our Lord Jesus Christ, that
though he was rich, yet for your sakes he became poor,
that ye through his poverty might be rich."   " If any
man hath not the spirit of Christ, he is none of his."
Also the riches of God's goodness and forbearance
and long-suffering should lead us to repentance and
provoke us unto good works.

There are many other passages of the Bible that
should edify.   Prov. xi. 24, 25: " There is that scat-
tereth, and yet increaseth; and there is that withhold-
eth more than is meet, but it tendeth to poverty.   The
liberal soul shall be made fat: and he that watereth
shall be watered also himself."   This promises a reward for charity to the poor and liberality to the
Church, but declares adversity to the contracted mind.

The Jews had withheld their support and offerings
from the temple until the service and worship of God
were neglected and looked upon with disfavor.   In
Mal. iii. 8-11 God in pity warns them, and offers mercy
and great blessings if they will return to duty: " Will
a man rob God?   Yet ye have robbed me.   . . .
In tithes and offerings.   Ye are cursed with a curse:
for ye have robbed me, even this whole nation.   Bring
ye all the tithes into the storehouse, that there may be
meat in mine house, and prove me now herewith, saith
the Lord of hosts, if I will not open you the windows
of heaven, and pour you out a blessing, that there
shall not be room enough to receive it."   If a man
robs God, he would, with favorable opportunity, rob

men.   He has the disposition; yet God is merciful, and
offers pardon.   Such blessings were only promised on
condition of their bringing the required support to the
worship of God.   So he deals with us to-day.   The
principles of his government are always the same.   2
Cor. ix. 6-8: "He which soweth sparingly shall reap
also sparingly; and he which soweth bountifully shall
reap also bountifully.   Every man according as he
purposeth in his heart, so let him give; not grudgingly,
or of necessity: for God loveth a cheerful giver.   And
God is able to make all grace abound toward you; that
ye, always having all sufficiency in all things, may
abound to every good work."   Is that not fair, just,
and liberal toward us?   Then is it not clearly *dishonest* when we want so many blessings from God, *bountiful* reaping, while we sow *sparingly?*   Besides, we
often contribute "grudgingly, or of necessity," while
God demands that we give heartily.   He "loveth a
cheerful giver."

In Matt. xxv. appears the parable of talents.   The
"man" intrusted his goods to servants.   To one he
gave five talents; to another, two; and to another, one.
The man, on his return, had a reckoning with the servants.   Two of them had been equally faithful with
different trusts, so they received equal rewards.   The
third had hid his master's money in the earth, and never used it.   His lord said: "Take the talent from him,
and give it unto him which hath ten talents.   For
unto every one that hath shall be given, and he shall
have abundance; but from him that hath not shall be
taken away even that which he hath.   And cast ye the
unprofitable servant into outer darkness: there shall
be weeping and gnashing of teeth."

In Luke xix. appears the parable of pounds.   The
"nobleman" intrusted to each of his ten servants one
pound.   On his return they made report.   They had

been differently faithful with equal trusts, hence their master rewarded those who had increased his goods differently and according to their fidelity; but upon the servant who hid his pound in a napkin and returned it entire he pronounced a rebuke. The unfaithful servant in each parable was not charged with murder, not even with dishonesty. Each was charged of sin, in that he did *nothing* in the service of his master, and was punished for it.

Christ teaches in these parables that God will so deal with *all* who are now doing as those servants did.

5

CHAPTER VII.

EXCUSES.

WE often hear from certain kinds of people excuses for not paying to the support of the Church, such as: " It costs too much to run the Church now, much more than in old times." It seems that the reason of such men is lost in their stinginess, specially with the Church. The Church does cost more, but it accomplishes more. Would we have the Church return to the slow pace of former times in this country? " The preacher has not visited me." " Our pastor can't *preach.*" " Our preacher neglects his work." Suppose all that be true, the members owe so much to the Church, not to the preacher. The Church owes the preacher. Has a citizen a right to refuse to pay taxes to civil government because the money he pays in will help support a civil officer he objects to? The civil law forces him to do his part. He takes advantage of the Church because no law compels him to pay. An honorable man will try to do right without coercion from any law. " The preacher wears fine clothes, bought with our money we made by hard work. Let *him* work." Why not exact the same of your lawyer or physician? Suppose they spend in farm work the time needed in cultivation of a crop and care of a farm, what kind of lawyers and physicians would you have? " The preacher has more money than I have now." " He doesn't need money, anyway." Suppose that be true, and that your preacher be worth a million of dollars, have you a right to withhold the wages of a man who labors on your farm or in your shop or store, or withhold money you owe your merchant on the ground that he is now

(60)

worth more than you? If that be dishonest, it is as bad to treat your preacher so. "He has a better horse and buggy than I have now." You should be glad of it. You may *never* own a horse or a buggy. Your want of one may be from choice or lack of enterprise. Would you have him hampered in his work by having to walk or by driving an old, worn-out horse to a worn-out buggy? If that suited your taste, how would it suit that of hundreds of others? A preacher should be well equipped in every way for his work, and prepared, by neat dress and every other proper means, to enter any good society and any home. "I don't like the assessment plan; it is a tax." It is not an exaction, merely an apportionment by the stewards to be consented to by the members. No Church without such system ever approaches its duty. The success of all that try this plan declares its efficiency; and I believe in nearly or quite all cases the objection is a mere subterfuge. Some croakers threaten to leave the Church when any spirit of progress is shown. Don't be frightened, brethren. Their withdrawal will not destroy the Church. Let such men go. In the Church they would forever obstruct progress. Let them go, or, if they prefer continuing in our Church, never be influenced by their depressing words or example.

"Hard times. We must put our pastor's salary low, and let him bear the burden with his people." That is a plausible excuse; but the people of this country have never known hard times to justify this plea. The salaries of our preachers are already small in the most flourishing times, and, when apportioned among the members, hardly any one is asked to pay enough for it to be *any sacrifice;* yet the aggregate of what all could easily do any year would furnish a comfortable support and respectable salary for their preacher.

" Hard times. I need the money myself; can't give it to the Church." I say *"give."* You *owe* it to God, my friend.

The following story was taken from the *Union Gospel News:* "A prosperous member of a Church in Scotland was often besought by his pastor to give to the work of evangelizing the poor in Glasgow, but would always reply: ' Na; I need it for mysel'.' One night he dreamed that he was at the gate of heaven, which was only a few inches ajar. He tried to get in, but could not, and was in agony at his poor prospect. The face of his minister appeared, who said: ' Sandy, why stand ye glowering there? Why don't ye gae in?' ' I can't; I am too large, and my pocketbook sticks out whichever way I turn.' ' Sandy, think how mean you have been to the Lord's poor, and ye will grow small to go through the eye of a needle.' He awoke, and began to reduce both his pocketbook and his carnality by giving to Christ's cause."

CHAPTER VIII.

WHATEVER may be our personal opinions and excuses for failure, let us consult the " law and the testimony." That should be recognized as a " lamp unto our feet, and a light unto our path."

The Levites were chosen of God to do the ordinary services about the temple, thus assisting the priests. For this they received tithes of the heave offerings, and no other inheritance among the people; and of this they were to give a tenth. Num. xviii. 20-26: " The Lord spake unto Aaron, Thou shalt have no inheritance in their land, neither shalt thou have any part among them: I am thy part and thine inheritance among the children of Israel. And, behold, I have given the children of Levi all the tenth in Israel for an inheritance, for their service which they serve, even the service of the tabernacle of the congregation. . . . The tithes of the children of Israel, which they offer as a heave offering unto the Lord, I have given unto the Levites to inherit. . . . And the Lord spake unto Moses, saying, Thus speak unto the Levites, and say unto them, When ye take of the children of Israel the tithes which I have given you from them for your inheritance, then ye shall offer up a heave offering of it for the Lord, even a tenth part of the tithe." Our preachers now, as a body, are the most liberal men in the world. Deut. xviii. 1-5: "And this shall be the priest's due from the people, from them that offer a sacrifice, whether it be ox or sheep; and they shall give unto the priest the shoulder, and the two cheeks, and the maw. The first fruit also of thy corn, of thy

(63)

wine [it was not intoxicating wine], and of thine oil, and the first of the fleece of thy sheep, shalt thou give him. For the Lord thy God hath chosen him out of all thy tribes, to stand to minister in the name of the Lord, him and his sons forever." Many put this debt *last*, but God says " *first* " in time and choice. Why does God so rate this obligation? Read again Deut. xviii. 5: " For the Lord thy God hath chosen him . . . to minister *in the name* of the Lord." They are *messengers* of God on important business to *you, all for you*. " Hold such in reputation." " Esteem them very highly in love *for their work's sake*." Nehemiah (xiii. 10, 11) said: " I perceived that the portions of the Levites had not been given them: for the Levites and the singers, that did the work [in the temple], were fled every one to his field [for support]. Then contended I with the rulers, and said, Why is the house of God forsaken?" Nehemiah renewed the service. God had been displeased, and there was spiritual death until they returned to God's plan. God promises blessings conditionally. (Read Mal. iii. 10.)

Rev. C. O. Jones, of Texas, said: "Any man who promises to pay so much to the Church, and then, because of some objection to the preacher, or other trivial excuse, refuses, is dishonest; and he would not pay other debts if he were not compelled by law. Any one who is financially able, yet will not promise and will not pay, ought to be expelled from the Church for lying; for he vowed to support the institutions of the Church."

Among other directions Christ gave the apostles when he sent them out, he said (Matt. x. 9, 10): "Provide neither gold, nor silver, nor brass in your purses, nor scrip for your journey, neither two coats, neither shoes, nor yet staves: for the workman is worthy of his meat." This tells the people their duty, and it is to Christ's ministers a promise of his special providence. Many preachers at the close of the year cannot understand how they lived on such small salary. Luke x. 7: "The laborer is worthy of his hire." Read all of 1 Cor. ix. 1-14. I quote a part of it: "Who goeth a warfare any time at his own charges? who planteth a vineyard, and eateth not of the fruit thereof? or who feedeth a flock, and eateth not of the milk of the flock? . . . It is written in the law of Moses, Thou shalt not muzzle the mouth of the ox that treadeth out the corn. . . . For our sakes, no doubt, this is written: that he that ploweth should plow in hope; and that he that thrasheth in hope should be partaker of his hope. If we have sown unto you spiritual things, is it a great thing if we shall reap your carnal things? . . . Do ye not know that they which minister about holy things live of the things of the temple? and they which wait at the altar are partakers with the altar? Even so hath the Lord ordained that they which preach the gospel should live of the gospel." Can language be plainer than this? Yet Paul preached to the Corinthians without charge, lest they might think he was seeking theirs rather than them. Still he suspected this was not best for them, and wrote them: "Forgive me this wrong." (See 2 Cor. xii. 13, 14.)

Gal. vi. 6: "Let him that is taught in the word communicate unto him that teacheth in all good things."

In the face of all such scripture teachings, many a member says, "I just can't raise the money to pay my preacher," or church dues, and yet offers no complaint in paying his lodge dues for fear he may be suspended for nonpayment.

David went up to buy the thrashing floor of Arau-

nah to offer sacrifice.   Araunah offered to give to the
king all that was desired for the worship.   David said:
" Nay,   .   .   .   neither will I offer burnt offerings
unto the Lord my God of that which doth cost me
nothing."   Noble spirit!   Talk about " up-to-date "
Christians, some people are lagging *far behind* David;
and he offered this sacrifice to God two thousand nine
hundred and fourteen years ago.

Let all the people sing:

> Here I give my all to thee—
> Friends and time and earthly store;
> Soul and body thine to be,
> Wholly thine for evermore.